My Thankful Journal

For Kids

Giving Thanks Day by Day

Deborah Haddix

My Thankful Journal for Kids: Giving Thanks Day by Day
Copyright ©2020 by Deborah Haddix
All rights reserved.

Requests for information should be sent to:
Deborah Haddix
P.O. Box 8293
West Chester, OH 45069
www.deborahhaddix.com

ISBN: 9798551578055

For:
Emma, Logan, Olivia, Sadie, Belle, Casen, Owen, Aubree, Nora, Beckett, Kylah, and Sutton

Contents

Giving Thanks Day by Day

Give thanks to the God of gods,

for his steadfast love endures forever.

Give thanks to the Lord of lords,

for his steadfast love endures forever.

Psalm 136:2-3

A Note to Parents

Are you searching for ways to help your child grow in gratitude?

My Thankful Journal for Kids is a tool you can use to help your child practice the act of giving thanks, and as we know some things simply take lots of practice. As you work through the journal as a family, your children will be guided to read about, discuss, and reflect upon specific things for which to be thankful.

Included in this journal are twenty-seven days of "thankful" activities. If further practice is desired following completion of the journal activities, a list of suggested follow-up activities is provided. It is my hope these activities will assist you and your children in thinking through and talking together about how wonderful our Lord is and that they will provide meaningful practice that will develop into an attitude of gratitude.

Welcome

Welcome to My Thankful Journal for Kids!

Did you know that God tells us to be thankful?

"[Give] thanks always and for everything to God the Father
in the name of our Lord Jesus Christ."
Ephesians 5:20

Look back up at that verse again. Do you see those words – "always" and "for everything?" I don't know about you, but if I am honest, sometimes I find it difficult to be thankful "always" and "for everything."

Oh, it's pretty easy to be thankful for a special gift like a new bicycle or a huge surprise such as a trip to Disney, but being thankful when your brother eats the last cookie on the plate is not so easy. Is it? We would rather feel sorry for ourselves or be angry, because we did not get to eat the cookie.

Being thankful all the time, no matter what, takes work. It does not come naturally to us. We want things to go our way, and often we are so busy we do not even think about giving thanks.

That is what this book is about – helping you to slow down and practice giving thanks. Each day you will read a Bible verse, think about it, make a journal entry, and end in prayer. As you work through the book, I pray the practice will help you develop an ongoing attitude of gratitude –

"Giving thanks always and for everything to God the Father in the name of our Lord Jesus Christ."
Ephesians 5:20

Giving Thanks

Day by Day

Day 1

 READ: Ephesians 5:20

"Giving thanks always and for everything to God the Father in the name of our Lord Jesus Christ."

 THINK: Wow! Do you get what that verse is saying?

Go back and read it again. This time draw a line under the word that tells us WHEN we are supposed to give thanks. Then draw two lines under the word that tells us what we are to give thanks for.

"Always" and "for everything." Sometimes that can be very hard for us to do. But this verse means that we are to be thankful for the big things, the little things, the good things, and, yes, even the bad things in our lives.

 JOURNAL: What are you thankful for? Take a few minutes. Think about the big things, the little things, the good things, and the not-so-good things. Then on your journal page, list or draw at least five things for which you are thankful.

 PRAY: With a thankful heart, thank God for each item on your list.

Day 2

 READ: Matthew 19:13-14

"Then children were brought to him that he might lay his hands on them and pray. The disciples rebuked the people, but Jesus said, 'Let the little children come to me and do not hinder them, for to such belongs the kingdom of heaven.'"

THINK: Do you know what the word "rebuke" means? It means to express harsh disapproval.

The disciples did not approve of the people bringing their children to Jesus, and they got after them for doing so. Apparently, the disciples thought Jesus was too busy for children.

Have you ever felt like someone was too busy for you? I know I have. Isn't it wonderful to know that Jesus is never too busy or too tired to spend time with His children? He loves you with a love that always welcomes you.

 JOURNAL: Take some time to thank Jesus for loving you and always having time for you. On your journal page, write a thank you note to Him.

PRAY: Read your note out loud to Jesus as a prayer.

Dear Jesus,

_____

_____

_____

_____

_____

_____

_____

_____

_____

_____

_____

_____

_____

Love,

Day 3

 READ: Psalm 30:4

"Sing praises to the Lord, O you his saints, and give thanks to his holy name."

THINK: God's name is holy. This means that His name is special and set apart from others.

Did you know that there are several names used for God in the Bible? You will find some of these names on your journal page for today. Go ahead; take a look at them before you read on.

Each of these names for God that we find in Scripture reveals something about His character. They are windows into who He is and what He is like.

JOURNAL: Choose one or more of the names of God on your journal page and write about it. What does the name mean to you? What do you already know about this name? What would you like to learn about the name? Finally, on the bottom of the page, thank God for this name and what it means about Him.

PRAY: Bow your head in an act of reverence (respect and awe) and thank God for His holy name.

YHWH – *I AM*   *El Roi* – *The God Who Sees Me*

Adonai – *The Lord*   *Jehovah Jireh* – *My Provider*

Elohim – *My Creator*   *El Shaddai* – *My supplier*

Ancient of Days   *Abba*

Thank you, God, for Your name _____ .

Day 4

 READ: Psalm 7:17

"I will give to the Lord the thanks due to his righteousness, and I will sing praise to the name of the Lord, the Most High."

THINK: "Righteousness." That is a really big word we don't use much in our everyday conversations. If you look in a dictionary, you might find that it means being upright in character, living by the principles of right conduct, or knowing right from wrong.

We may struggle in knowing right from wrong or making right choices sometimes, but God never does. He is perfect and righteous – all the time.

JOURNAL: Use your journal page to explore God's righteousness. Here are some ideas to help you get started.

- Look up synonyms for the word "righteous."
- Copy the definition onto your page.
- In your own words, describe what it means for God to be righteous.
- How do you feel when you think about God's righteousness?
- Write down any questions you have about God's righteousness.

PRAY: Thank God for His perfect righteousness. Talk to Him about the things you wrote on your journal page.

Day 5

 READ: Psalm 9:1

"I will give thanks to the Lord with my whole heart; I will recount all of your wonderful deeds."

THINK: Have you heard the old saying, "What's done is done?" When people say that they mean you can't change what happened in the past so put it behind you and move forward.

In a way they are right. You cannot change what happened in the past, and it is good to move forward. But we should not ignore the past completely.

God says in Psalm 98 that it is our duty to learn from the past. He wants us to look back on what we see Him do in the Bible and what we've seen Him do in our family so that we can learn more about who He is and avoid the mistakes others have made.

 JOURNAL: Think about God's wonderful deeds – the ones you see written in the Bible and the ones your family has experienced. With words or pictures make a list of all God's wonderful deeds that you can remember or choose just one deed in each column and write about it in as much detail as you can.

PRAY: Thankfully read your journal page to God as a prayer.

God's Wonderful Deeds in the Bible	God's Wonderful Deeds for My Family

Day 6

 READ: Psalm 28:7

"The Lord is my strength and my shield; in him my heart trusts, and I am helped; my heart exults, and with my song I give thanks to him."

THINK: Psalm 28 is a prayer. In the verses leading up to Psalm 28:7, we find a desperate David crying out to God for help. He is surrounded by wicked people who are pretending to be his friends but really want to ruin him.

But read verse 7 again. Do you see it? David does not keep crying and stay sad. He starts singing God's praise. Why? Because God is his strength (power) and his shield (protection). He knows he can trust God even when things are hard.

JOURNAL: There are so many ways you can journal your thanks to God for His power and protection. Choose one of the following or think of one of your own.

- What does the phrase "The Lord is my strength and my shield" mean to you?
- List or write about some of the things that make you feel sad or afraid. Then in a different color write the words "God I trust you with…" over top of your writing.
- Draw a picture of you, with God being your strength and shield.

PRAY: Read Psalm 28:7 to the Lord as a prayer; then thank Him for His power and protection over you. If you are struggling with something, end your prayer with, "Lord, I trust you with _____ *(fill in the blank with whatever you are struggling with)* ."

Day 7

READ: 1 Chronicles 16:34

"Oh give thanks to the Lord, for he is good; for his steadfast love endures forever!"

THINK: "An elephant never forgets!" Have you heard that before? It's an old saying some people use.

Scientists have proven that elephants do have incredible memories. (Maybe it is because they have large brains.) But they certainly cannot remember everything!

And neither do we. In fact, humans are quite forgetful. Besides forgetting to do our homework or where we put our shoes, we often fail to remember the millions and millions of ways God has been good to us.

The word "good" means to be morally excellent or virtuous. Those are big words, but they are very much like the word "righteous" that we looked at on Day 4. (You can go back and read it again if you like.)

Our verse today tells us God is good. He alone is without sin. He is the only One who is morally excellent and virtuous. Always right, everything God does is good.

 JOURNAL: Our verse today also tells us that we are to give thanks to God because He is good. On your journal page, list or draw the ways that God is good. Remember He is good in all He says and does.

PRAY: Pray in two parts today. First, confess (tell Him you are sorry) for taking His goodness for granted. Then, thank Him for the things on your list.

Day 8

 READ: James 1:17

"Every good gift and every perfect gift is from above, coming down from the Father of lights, with whom there is no variation or shadow due to change."

THINK: It may not always seem like it, but every person in the world has experienced goodness. Sometimes we take the good things we experience for granted. This means we just assume we will always have them, or we don't take time to appreciate them. There are even times when we do not pay any attention at all, ignoring the good things completely. And, sadly, there are times when we forget where the good things come from.

Read James 1:17 one more time. Where does it say the good things in our lives come from? That's right, from God who we already know is good.

JOURNAL: Today, let's pay attention and show appreciation for the good gifts God gives to us. Fill your journal page with good things you have enjoyed from God.

PRAY: Ask God to help you pay more attention to and be more appreciative of the good gifts he gives to you. Then thank Him for the "goodness" on your journal page.

Day 9

 READ: John 3:16 and Romans 6:23

"For God so loved the world, that he gave his only Son, that whoever believes in him should not perish but have eternal life."

"For the wages of sin is death, but the free gift of God is eternal life in Christ Jesus our Lord."

THINK: Let's take a closer look at today's verses. We'll start with John 3:16. Read it again and see if you can find the answers to these questions:

What gift did God give to the world?

Why did He give us this gift?

That's right! He gave His only Son, Jesus, so we can have eternal life.

Now look at Romans 6:23 and try to answer one more question:

How much does this wonderful gift cost us?

Right again! It does not cost us anything. It is FREE.

Does this blow your mind? The greatest gift ever, and it is free!

 JOURNAL: This free gift is the greatest demonstration of God's love and goodness toward us. There is no greater gift than the gift of Jesus and His work on the Cross. On your journal page, write a thank you note to God for this very special gift of His Son, Jesus.

PRAY: Read your thank you note to God as a prayer.

Dear God,

_____

_____

_____

_____

_____

_____

_____

_____

_____

_____

_____

_____

_____

_____

_____

_____

Love,

Day 10

 READ: Hebrews 4:12

"For the word of God is living and active, sharper than any two-edged sword, piercing to the division of soul and of spirit, of joints and of marrow, and discerning the thoughts and intentions of the heart."

THINK: Did you know the Bible is another name for "the word of God?" Today's verse could read, "For the Bible is living and active...."

The Bible is another wonderful gift that God has given to us.

Because God does not want us to live in darkness, He has chosen to reveal Himself to us through the Bible. This precious Book also contains everything we need to know about life and how to grow to be more like Christ.

JOURNAL: The Bible helps us in many ways. Some of the ways we are helped when we read it are listed on your journal page.

Read the list; then write your thoughts or questions about any of them in the space provided. When you are finished, go back and circle the ones that mean the most to you right now.

PRAY: Thank God for His Holy Word, the Bible. In your prayer, name some of the "helps" you circled.

The Bible...

Tells us how to be saved.
(John 3:16; Romans 10:9)

Guides our steps.
(Psalm 119:105)

Helps us gain understanding and wisdom. (Psalm 119:130)

Comforts us.
(Psalm 119:28)

Turns our focus back toward God.
(Psalm 119:37)

Fills us with hope.
(Psalm 119:49)

Inspires our praise.
(Psalm 119:62)

Reassures us.
(Psalm 119:75)

Brings us joy when we read it.
(Psalm 119:111)

Gives us peace.
(Psalm 119:165)

Strengthens us when we are tired.
(Psalm 119:107)

Day 11

 READ: Psalm 46:10

"Be still, and know that I am God."

THINK: Do you make pictures in your head when you read? I do. It's a great strategy for understanding what you read. Try it! Read Psalm 46:10 again, and this time picture it in your head as you read. What does your picture look like?

Did you notice that the verse says, "Be still," not "Sit still?"

Sitting still has to do with your body. It is the things you can see like fidgeting or messing with something. Being still has to do with your spirit. It's the things you cannot see deep inside you.

God speaks to our spirits, but we live in such a busy, noisy world that it can be very difficult for us to hear Him.

We like being busy and having lots of noise around us. It feels normal. We are not used to the quiet or to being still. It makes most of us feel very uncomfortable. But this is what God wants. He wants us to be still on the outside and the inside, so we can hear Him.

JOURNAL: Being still is a hard thing, but aren't you glad and thankful that the God of the universe wants to be with you and talk to you? In the first column on your journal page, list the things that make "being still" hard to do. In the second column, list some reasons that it is good to "be still" with God.

PRAY: "Dear God, help me to turn off the noise in my life and to be still with You. Thank you, that You want me to spend time with You. Amen."

THINGS THAT MAKE "BEING STILL" HARD	REASONS IT IS GOOD TO "BE STILL"

Day 12

 READ: 1 Corinthians 3:16 and 1 Corinthians 6:19

"Do you not know that you are God's temple and that God's Spirit dwells in you?"

"Or do you not know that your body is a temple of the Holy Spirit within you, whom you have from God? You are not your own."

THINK: The human body is an incredible machine. Made up of a head, neck, torso, two arms, and two legs, it is designed to stand, walk on two feet, carry things, and lift objects. All that, and it has thumbs that can grasp.

But wait! That's not all. Within the human body are many systems such as the digestive system and the central nervous system that give us the ability to move, think, grow, and live.

Have you ever stopped to think about what a remarkable gift your body is?

It is extraordinary, and we should do our best to take care of it. Afterall, we need to be in good shape when God wants to use us to serve others. And even more importantly, if we are believers in Christ, our body is His home.

JOURNAL: There are many ways to take care of our bodies such as eating correctly, resting properly, and exercising. Draw pictures or write about the ways you take care of your body. On your page include at least one thing you can do to better care for it.

PRAY: Thank God for your body. Ask Him how you can use it to serve others.

I can take better care of my body by:

Day 13

 READ: Genesis 1:27 and Psalm 94:9

"So God created man in his own image, in the image of God he created him; male and female he created them."

"He who planted the ear, does he not hear? He who formed the eye, does he not see?"

THINK: May I ask you a question? What is the most beautiful thing you have ever seen?

It's true, God gave us physical bodies that can do some amazing things like stand, walk, and carry things. But theses bodies can do so much more! They also help us "sense" the world around us. We have eyes to see, ears to hear, a nose to smell, a tongue to taste, and hands to touch.

JOURNAL: Let's concentrate on our eyes and ears. Stop, look, and listen. Write down or draw at least ten things that you can see right now and all the things you can hear.

PRAY: Thank God for your senses and the ability to see, hear, smell, taste, and touch. Thank Him, too, that He sees you and hears you just as it says in Psalm 94:9.

WHAT I CAN SEE

WHAT I CAN HEAR

Day 14

 READ: Daniel 2:23

"To you, O God of my fathers, I give thanks and praise, for you have given me wisdom and might, and have now made known to me what we asked of you, for you have made known to us the king's matter."

THINK: I once heard it said that "Knowledge is knowing that a tomato is fruit. Wisdom is knowing not to put it in a fruit salad." I'm not sure who said it, but this little saying stuck with me.

I think I like it because it is a little bit funny and makes the important point that knowledge and wisdom are not the same thing.

The big difference between those two words is that knowledge is simply "knowing" information and wisdom is knowing "how to use" what you know.

Today's verse tells us that God gives us wisdom.

JOURNAL: On your journal page, make a list of things you would like to "know" more about. Then write your thoughts and questions about the difference in knowing something and exercising "wisdom" with what you know.

PRAY: Thank God for the ability to think and learn. Thank Him for the knowledge you have and ask Him to help you grow in wisdom.

Day 15

 READ: Matthew 15:29 and Mark 6:31

"Jesus went on from there and walked beside the Sea of Galilee. And he went up on the mountain and sat down there."

"And he said to them, 'Come away by yourselves to a desolate place and rest a while.' For many were coming and going, and they had no leisure even to eat."

THINK: I do not know very many kids who like to take naps. Most don't even want to sit down and be still for one single minute. But rest is important.

Did you know even Jesus rested! During His ministry on the earth, there were times when Jesus felt the need for rest. He knew that His body and His spirit needed it. It was so necessary to Him that He sometimes left important work to go get rest. From time to time, He even made His disciples stop working so they could rest.

Rest time, naps, and a good night's sleep give us energy for when we are awake. Think about some of the ways that getting rest helps us.

JOURNAL: Write down three or four ways that rest helps our bodies. Then write down three or four things that could happen if we do not get enough rest.

PRAY: Thank God that in His wisdom He thought of providing ways for our bodies to rest.

When I am rested:

When I don't get enough rest:

Day 16

 READ: Genesis 1:1 and Psalm 102:25

"In the beginning, God created the heavens and the earth."

"Of old you laid the foundation of the earth, and the heavens are the work of your hands."

THINK: Close your eyes and try to "picture" NOTHING. It's very hard, isn't it? How do we picture "absolute nothingness" when we are so used to being surrounded by all manner of things?

The Bible tells us that God created the heavens and the earth. The word, *create*, means to make something from nothing. God spoke, and where there had been nothing, suddenly there was something.

JOURNAL: Look outside. Do you see some of the "something" God created? On your journal page, list or draw at least five things you see that were created by God.

PRAY: Whisper a prayer of thanksgiving to God for His work of creation. In your prayer, mention some of the things on your list.

Day 17

 READ: Genesis 1:5 and Psalm 118:24

"God called the light Day, and the darkness he called Night. And there was evening and there was morning, the first day."

"This is the day that the Lord has made; let us rejoice and be glad in it."

THINK: On the first day of creation, God created day and night. How wonderful He is to meet our every need. The first thing He did was give us nights so we can rest our minds and bodies and days so we can use our rested minds and bodies for His glory.

Aren't new days wonderful? Each one holds opportunities for us to serve God and be a blessing to others. And one more thing I like about them is that new days always give me a chance to start over if I am having a hard time or feeling like I messed up.

JOURNAL: What do you like about new days? Whatever it is, write about it on your journal page. Then think of at least one thing you can do today to bless someone else and write it down. Now, with your parent's permission, go do it!

PRAY: If you are able, go outside into the light of day and look up toward heaven. Thank God for new days and "start-overs." Ask Him to help you use this day to His glory and the blessing of someone else.

Day 18

 READ: Genesis 1:14 and Genesis 8:22

"And God said, "Let there be lights in the expanse of the heavens to separate the day from the night. And let them be for signs and for seasons, and for days and years."

"While the earth remains, seedtime and harvest, cold and heat, summer and winter, day and night, shall not cease."

THINK: Do you live in an area of the world where you get to experience all four seasons? I do, and while winter is not my favorite season, I cannot imagine living where I do not get to see snow.

I thank God for creating the seasons. Each one is unique and surrounds us with a beauty all its own. Do you have a favorite season, or do you love them all equally?

JOURNAL: On your journaling page, draw a picture to match each season or list things specific to each.

PRAY: Share with God what you enjoy about each of the seasons. Remember to thank Him for the beauty and uniqueness He created for us.

Spring

Summer

Fall

Winter

Day 19

 READ: Genesis 1:11 and Genesis 1:24

"And God said, 'Let the earth sprout vegetation, plants yielding seed, and fruit trees bearing fruit in which is their seed, each according to its kind, on the earth.' And it was so."

"And God said, 'Let the earth bring forth living creatures according to their kinds—livestock and creeping things and beasts of the earth according to their kinds.' And it was so."

THINK: One of my favorite names for God is Creator! One spring when we were driving through Pennsylvania, my granddaughters and I marveled at how many different types of trees we saw. And you know what? As we continued to drive, our gaze moved to the leaves of those trees where we saw even more variety in all the amazing shades of green.

God certainly created a well thought out world that meets our needs and allows us to live, but He went so far beyond that creating a world full of beauty for us to enjoy.

Trees and animals are wonderful examples of God's beauty and variety on display. Did you know there are at least twenty-four varieties of trees and forty different types of animals mentioned in the Bible? Think about all the types of animals just in the region where you live or at your nearby zoo.

 JOURNAL: On your journal page, list or draw the animals and trees that fit each category. In the fourth spot, record things that come in several varieties just like trees and animals.

PRAY: Thank God for variety.

Animals That Live
in My Region

Animals That Do Not
Live in My Region

Trees in My Neighborhood

Things That Come in
Many Varieties

47

Day 20

 READ: Genesis 2:24 and Proverbs 17:6

"Therefore a man shall leave his father and his mother and hold fast to his wife, and they shall become one flesh."

"Grandchildren are the crown of the aged, and the glory of children is their fathers."

 THINK: Family is a special blessing given to us by God.

We have talked about how God the Creator spoke this magnificent world into being and all the wonder, beauty, and variety it holds. But the masterpiece of Creation, the one that reveals more about God than anything else, is family.

When God created the family, He provided us with a place to learn and grow. Members of a family teach and serve one another. They share all of life's joys and sorrows. Family is important because it provides love and support to each of its members. Even more than all that, this special creation called family reflects the character of God and provides a safe place where we can experience His love.

Have you ever thought about the fact that even Jesus was born into a family? While He lived on this earth, He submitted to an earthly mom and dad to model what it means to honor parents and to benefit from their care and direction (Luke 2:52).

JOURNAL: Draw a picture of your family and list your favorite things about being a member or write about the importance of family and how it reflects God's character.

PRAY: Thank God for His masterpiece called family and all the benefits it provides to us. Thank Him for your own family and ask Him to help you better honor your parents.

Day 21

 READ: Proverbs 17:17 and John 15:12-13

"A friend loves at all times."

""My command is this: Love each other as I have loved you. Greater love has no one than this: to lay down one's life for one's friends."

THINK: Next to having a saving relationship with Christ there is nothing much better than having a friend. We need friends, and they need us.

A godly friend will be honest with you and tell you the truth, even if it hurts. They will go out of their way for you and love you no matter what. They do these things because they want to help you grow to become more and more like Christ.

JOURNAL: To have a friend, we must be a friend. How can you be a friend to someone? Think of three ways you can show friendship to someone. Write them on your journal page. Then in the space provided, list the names of your godly friends.

PRAY: Thank God for your godly friends. If you need a godly friend, ask Him for one. Then ask Him to help you be a friend to others.

THANK YOU FOR MY GODLY FRIENDS:

Day 22

 READ: Psalm 92:1 and Psalm 100:4

"It is good to give thanks to the LORD, to sing praises to your name, O Most High."

"Enter his gates with thanksgiving, and his courts with praise! Give thanks to him; bless his name!"

THINK: How does Psalm 92:1 begin? That's right! "It is good to give thanks to the LORD."

Say that out loud three times. Now, one more time, loudly and with lots of feeling! Do you believe it?

God wants us to have a thankful heart. Some people call this an attitude of gratitude. This does not come easily to most of us. It is something we have to work at. One way to develop an attitude of gratitude is to write down things you are thankful for every day. You can try this by putting a pencil and a little notebook by your bed and writing your "thankful list" before you climb in bed each night.

JOURNAL: Start your "thankful list" on today's journal page. Draw or list at least five things you are thankful for. Come back any time and add things to your list.

PRAY: "God, the Bible says it is good to give thanks to You. Please help me develop an attitude of gratitude." (Then thank Him for the things on your journal page.)

Day 23

 READ: Psalm 109:30

"With my mouth I will give great thanks to the Lord; I will praise him in the midst of the throng."

THINK: Our verse today comes from the very end of Psalm 109. This Psalm is a prayer that was prayed by David.

Once again in an extremely difficult situation where people are trying to hurt him, David begins his prayer by asking God for help. Then in the middle of his prayer, he even calls on God to judge those who are against him. But as sad and afraid as he is, David ends his prayer with a promise to use his mouth to praise God and give Him thanks.

Do you use your mouth to say thank you to God?

JOURNAL: Write a thank you note to God. In your note, name some specific things you want to thank Him for.

PRAY: Use your mouth to say, "thank you," to God. Read your thank you note out loud to Him as a prayer.

Dear God,

_____

_____

_____

_____

_____

_____

_____

_____

_____

_____

_____

_____

_____

_____

Love,

Day 24

 READ: Psalm 138:1 and Psalm 86:12

"I give you thanks, O Lord, with my whole heart; before the gods I sing your praise."

"I give thanks to you, O Lord my God, with my whole heart, and I will glorify your name forever."

THINK: Do you know who wrote Psalm 138 and Psalm 86? That's right! David!

Yesterday, we read about David promising to thank God with his mouth. Now in these verses, we see David giving thanks to God with his whole heart. Have you ever thought about giving thanks to God with your whole heart? What do you think that would look like?

Here are some ideas I have when I read today's verses. I think giving thanks with our whole heart means we will be eager to say thank you and do it cheerfully. A thank you given with our whole heart will be real and honest, not fake. It means I will really mean it when I say thank you.

What are some ideas you have about giving thanks with our whole heart?

JOURNAL: On your journal page, write down what you think it means to thank God with your whole heart.

PRAY: Using your journal page as a reminder if you need to, thank God with your whole heart.

Day 25

 READ: 1 Thessalonians 5:18

"Give thanks in all circumstances; for this is the will of God in Christ Jesus for you."

THINK: Today's verse tells us to "give thanks in all circumstances." Do you know what that means?

"Circumstances" mean all the things going on around you or happening to you. So, this verse says, "Give thanks no matter what is going on around you or happening to you."

Good things, bad things, happy things, sad things – God's will for us is that we be thankful no matter what!

JOURNAL: In the column on the left side of your page, make a list with words or pictures of times when you do not feel like saying thank you to God. Then in the other column, make a list of the times when you do feel like thanking God.

PRAY: Ask God to help you give thanks with your whole heart even when you do not feel like it. During your prayer, share your lists with Him. When you are finished, go back and draw a big black "X" over the "Do Not Feel Like It" list.

WHEN I DO NOT FEEL
LIKE THANKING GOD

WHEN I DO FEEL
LIKE THANKING GOD

Day 26

 READ: Colossians 3:17 and Ephesians 5:20

"And whatever you do, in word or deed, do everything in the name of the Lord Jesus, giving thanks to God the Father through him."

"Giving thanks always and for everything to God the Father in the name of our Lord Jesus Christ."

 THINK: Everything you do is to be done in the name of Christ. Just to be sure you didn't miss it, read Colossians 3:17 one more time. This time use your pencil to underline the words that tell you this.

"Everything" – eating, sleeping, doing schoolwork, taking out the trash, sweeping the floor, dance practice, football drills, obeying parents – is to be done in the name of Christ.

Giving thanks can also go in our list of "everything." So, we are to give thanks to God in Jesus' name. Just like we pray in Jesus' name, we are to give thanks to God in His name.

JOURNAL: Give thanks "to God the Father in the name of our Lord Jesus Christ."

PRAY: Use your journal page to pray a thank you prayer to God the Father.

Father God,

In the name of our Lord Jesus Christ, I thank you for...

Day 27

 READ: Psalm 95:2 and Ephesians 5:19-20

"Let us come into his presence with thanksgiving; let us make a joyful noise to him with songs of praise!"

"Singing and making melody to the Lord with your heart, giving thanks always and for everything to God the Father in the name of our Lord Jesus Christ."

THINK: Psalm 95:2 says, "Let us come into his presence with thanksgiving." That verb "come" means "to go to meet God, to be in His presence" – face-to-face.

As we end our day-by-day giving of thanks to God, remember that you are invited to meet God face-to-face with your thanksgiving.

JOURNAL: Thank God that because of Jesus' finished work on the Cross, you are invited into His presence, where you can meet Him face-to-face anytime.

PRAY: With a joyful heart (and some joyful noise), "sing" a prayer of thanksgiving to God. Thank God for… Jesus' obedience in dying on the Cross for you, His resurrection, and that He lives today. Thank Him that you can go to meet Him, be in His presence face-to-face, and offer a song of thanksgiving.

Conclusion

Wow! I wish I could be right there sitting beside you to give you a big high-five! You just finished twenty-seven days of giving thanks to God. Your dedication to finishing the job you started is reason to celebrate.

Now, as we are celebrating, let me ask you an important question: "Where will you go from here?"

With your day-by-day practice of the last few weeks, you are well on your way to establishing a habit of giving thanks – a healthy habit you want to continue developing. While it is on your mind, talk to your parents and make a plan for how you will continue to grow an attitude of gratitude in your heart.

If you need some help getting started, here are a few suggestions:

- Read through the Suggested Follow-up Activities with your parents and choose one. You can do it by yourself or as a family.
- Each month choose a new activity from the list and do it to keep your habit growing.
- Use the Personal Thanksgiving Pages at the end of this book to keep an ongoing list of things you are thankful for. Add to your list regularly.
- Write thank-you notes to God on the Personal Thanksgiving Pages.

No matter how you decide to grow your attitude of gratitude, keep your healthy habit going – for "it is good to give thanks to the Lord" (Psalm 92:1).

Suggested Follow-up Activities

Thankful ABC's

Write the alphabet, from A to Z, down the side of your paper. Then for each letter, write or draw something you are thankful that begins with that letter.

Thankful Box

Decorate a special "Thankful Box." Each day write down something for which you are thankful and place it in the box. Schedule a night for a "Thankful Dinner" or "Thankful Celebration" where the box is opened, and each slip of paper is read aloud.

Thankful Calendar

On your family calendar or a special calendar chosen for just this purpose, write down something each day for which you are thankful. This can be done individually or as a family. Do not let a day go by without adding your "thanks." At the end of the year, you will have a calendar holding your 365 days-worth of thanks.

Thankful Journal

Create your own individual or family "Thankful Journal." Write down or draw pictures of things you are thankful for. Be sure to make an entry in the journal each day. Set aside a special time to read through your journal.

Thankful Prayer

Choose one day of the week and make it "Thankful Prayer" day. On that day, say a prayer to God where all you do is thank Him. Do not ask for anything. Be specific with your thanks.

Thank You Notes

Make it a habit to send a thank you note to at least one person you know each week. Be sure to thank them for something specific. If you make the thank you note yourself, it will be even more special.

Personal Thanksgiving Pages

"You are my God, and I will give thanks to you;

you are my God; I will extol you."

Psalm 118:28

Books on Giving Thanks

All Creatures Great and Small (Board Book) by Naoko Stoop (Illustrator)

God Gave Us Thankful Hearts by Lisa Tawn Bergren

Grateful (Picture Book with Accompanying CD) by John Bucchino

Grateful Together: A Gratitude Journal for Kids and Their Parents by Vicky Perreault

Gratitude Journal & Devotional for Kids by Jessica Lewis

My Attitude of Gratitude by Melissa Winn

Thankful (Board Book) by Eileen Spinelli

Thank You, God (Board Book) by P.K. Hallinan

The Blessings Jar (Board Book) by Colleen Coble

Other Resources by Deborah Haddix

Faith Journaling for Kids: An Adventure in Creatively Connecting with God - Journaling is a spiritual discipline that reaps bountiful rewards for all who use it. Sadly, however, kids are often overlooked when we talk about or teach this valuable discipline. Faith Journaling is an adventure just for them, providing kids with examples and practice exercises in several types of faith journaling including prayer, Scripture, thanks, and more.

Digging Deeper KIDS (3 Options)

- Digging Deeper KIDS Methods includes 9 different techniques for helping children engage with the Word of God.

- Kids' Journaling Templates are perfect for the child who is intimidated by a blank page or as "training wheels" for the Digging Deeper Kids Methods.

- The Digging Deeper Kids BUNDLE includes both The Digging Deeper Methods AND The Digging Deeper Journaling Templates.

Scripture Journaling Workbook – A basic *"how-to"* of Scripture Journaling. Includes creative lettering tips and practice in creative doodling and lettering.

Journaling for the Soul: A Handbook — The busyness of life has made its migration into the depths of our being, squeezing God out. Our soul cries out but the noise of life keeps it from being heard. *Journaling for the Soul* helps eliminate the hurry, brings quiet for hearing, and creates much needed space for soul work. This book includes a wide range of different methods to suit a variety personalities or seasons of life and topics: gratitude, simplicity, vision boards, timelines, journaling for friends, fears, self-reflection, attributes of God, names of Christ.

For more information on these and other resources by Deborah Haddix, visit deborahhaddix.com.

Made in the USA
Monee, IL
12 November 2020